POEMS FOR LYNN

Kenneth and Cheryl Lans

Kenneth Lans was born in Trinidad in the 1930s. He won the Madoo Exhibition Medal in 1941 - performing best among children his age in the national exam to enter secondary school.

His father did not allow him to finish Advanced Levels (something to do with his scholarship funding) which in turn meant no university degree which then affected his career advancement in the oil industry. Ken started his career in the oil industry as a trainee who was given all the available skills training and he worked his way up to Western District Superintendent at Texaco Trinidad Inc., Forest Reserve (in charge of the production fields on the west coast). In the late 1980s he was seconded to the smaller marine exploration company Trinmar in Point Fortin.

He took early retirement and went to live in Tobago; which turned out to be a wise move since he died from cancer-related causes shortly after his sixty-fifth birthday and would not have had any retirement at all if he had waited.

He was delighted with his Apple computer and used it to write short stories and poems from 1990 – 1994, including these. A faithful husband who writes you romantic poems after retirement; what more could a woman want?

Cheryl, Ken's elder daughter has conducted research on medicinal plants and has published two books and several research papers that are available on Pubmed. The photocollages in this book were done by Cheryl Lans using public sources including Wikipedia.

Contents

A TALE OF NIGHT SAUCES

How great is my life ever since I've found peace of mind with my whole body sound! When I survey the wonders I have wrought,
The results justify the means and the thought.
Ruler! Supreme in My enchanted garden,
I suffer no one here to remain harden[1].

My plants are my children, all blooming and bright, with marvellous flowers, blossoms and buds, To delight all my friends and my minions are so few. The few things missing I shall never rue!

Rosebushes have thorns, those pricks I do fear, for by any other name is pickas[2] I still hear! Subtly sweet are the fragrances where'er I walk.
Softly whisper the leaves as they exchange old talk, with gossipy breezes rustling among the branches,
Causing endless play of light and shadows, while the benign sun shuffles through the hollows, amused no doubt by efforts seeming ever so grand to me, Empress over all this enchanted land!

Today has been lovely and was really worthwhile,
Tonight there is no moon I'll be dreaming in style!
Befitting one possessed with so many blessings

---

[1] Stubborn.
[2] thorn

That should I try to count them, my ears would ring
With hundreds, maybe thousands, perhaps even more!
I'm like the Twister Oliver, always asking for more!
Tonight by the window, I need not go
I've replaced the moon with one not so slow!
He I will see when I fall in sweet sleep
To dream of my fancies real and unreal,
And to roam the countryside, to go for my weal!

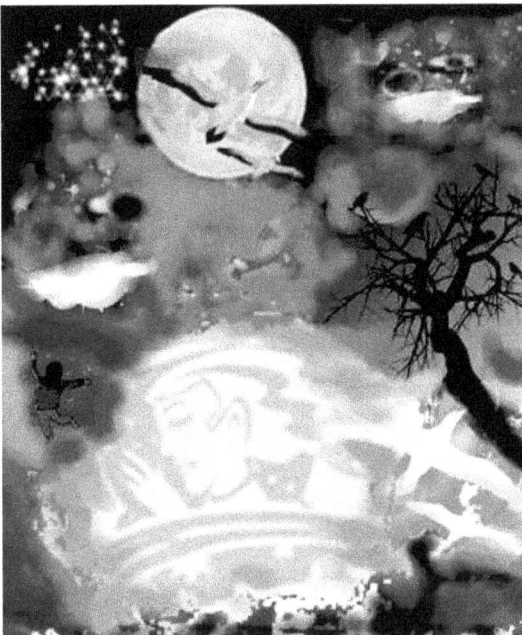

I have now no desire to share my throne, for that leads to fighting, like dogs o'er a bone. I feel really tired, and yet happily serene, because today I did as I liked, no holds were barred, And with some luck tonight I'll hold the trump card so close to my chest, that my lover's hands will roam yet once again, to give me so much pleasure, I would relish a little pain should it come after, For with it comes a sweet joy without measure!

One thing for sure, about all that you dream,
You can't get into trouble, no matter how wild
the scheme, or how creamy, or thick, or often,
the cream! With so much to gain and nothing to
lose, it's a wonderful time to do what you
choose!"

So off she went, Somnus hearkening to her call,

SOMNUS THE GOD OF SLEEP

Seeking romances, loves, trysts, and all experiences that had given her delight before! On her back with sweet lips forming a slight bore, through the open vent she did gamely snore! The whistling sounds alerted the fiends, Who on Dark Moon Night come out for their evil ends.

The devils, demons, imps, hob-goblins, all the mischievous elves hell-bent on deviltry, summoned with Black Magic, and sometimes with Obeah - a local variety! Around and around the bed they flew, curvetting with curtsies, and sprinkling drops of dew, Taken from some ancient witch's brew, on the sleeping figure so wrapped in slumber deep,

That all the caterwauling disturbed not her sleep! She was dreaming of her garden and of wetting her plants, with the fine measured shower rose, the only rose there, And she dreamt of a fine spray moistening her hair.

To their great dismay she paid them no heed!
Then they shook her bed with their might and their main
Seemingly to her she was driving her mechanical steed!
"I must get the shocks fixed they are bumpy hard again,"
Was her dream-thought, as they rattled her four-poster!

Their pranks were so unnoticed they got so extremely mad, that they called on their master to send someone really bad!

In a few seconds at their sides a shark materialized. He took one look and stood transfixed, as one hypnotized. "Not me and That One, No Way, Jose we tangled already, and she had all the play!

You fellow devils really lucky tonight, if she only look hard at you, all of you blight[3]! I taking sick leave, I have some days inside[4]. That Lady nearly take my manhood, and she already gone with my pride! So long fellas, I bid you farewell, my medicine to take down in Hell! You expect hell in Hell, but surely not here! Or is the place expanding, can anyone tell?"

"Go craven shark, you're just a herring to me, not even red, but yellow like a bee!" One devil taunted so loudly that her eyes opened wide, Though dreaming still, to fall upon Sharky's hide. "SO! Mr. Shark, You are Back once again?" BLOOD-FREEZING tones caused the heat-resistant imps, To shiver and hide behind the shark, like wimps!

"No, good lady, I mean you no harm! I was feeling very poorly, sick with ague, I've just come for some medicine to cure my flu!"

---

[3] unlucky
[4] Available days

"Oh! I see! And are those things behind your back,
The prescriptions you brought from the doctor Down There?"
She asked, her voice lowering icily once more.

They shivered and trembled, palsied with great fear,
As the temperature plunged, the mercury disappeared!
And all to a man thought, 'Sharky was right!
Let's get out of here! It's every man for himself! Let's dust from
this frightening place! Back to the devil we know, rather than face
the wrath of this woman still sound asleep!

Should she awake, we'll be in trouble too deep!
We know only to dish out, but never to take
The lumps and the bumps, the screams and the fears!'
"Well?" ..... she said quite threateningly.
"I'm a-waiting an answer, and no one dare leave,
Until I know what's going on beneath these eaves!"

One found his voice, and well-schooled in lying flattery said,
"We were passing on the way to the cemetery at Carnbee[5],
Your Majesty, when we saw your beautiful garden of flowers.
So entranced were we that we just had to bid
Goodnight to the owner, and I really must say
That we wasted precious time tonight
In the garden when we could have spent it
Watching the Fairest Flower of all festooned
With her creamy-white silks brocaded and trimmed,
In this lovely setting softly enhanced by lamp be-dimmed!"

---

[5] Carnbee is a town in *Tobago*, located about 5 kilometres southwest of Scarborough

"You're such a bloody liar, you surely were in politics in some life earlier, But you won't mamaguy[6] me! I know my way around your types, and all your dirty, scheming tricks! Now where is my BIBLE, and my Green PRAYER BOOK, My HOLY WATER, blessed by the priest, What's his name again? I have three large coloured candles consecrated at HOLY MASS, Those I will light to let this wicked dream pass"!

Shark Digestive System

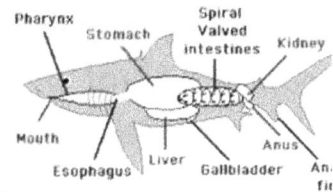

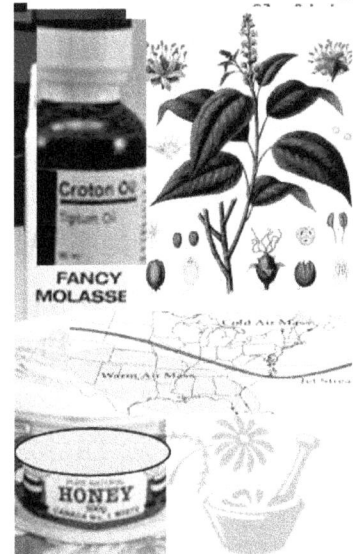

"As for you, Mr. Shark! I know what's ailing you! You've got both Die-er bite-es and High Blood pressure! So avoid drinking salt, keep away from Cod Liver and red meat for a while, Try cooler climes, where nearly all white is the style! Here is a glass of the medicine that you so rashly sought! It is Oils of Castor and of Crotons mixed with Senna, Molasses, Saccharin, and Honey laced with some Ferrol, to give you the strength to jet it out! This time it is for free, the treatment is on me, Your Kind of Money I don't need!

You will be a Jet-shark in no time at all! With so much speed your flu would have flown, In the trailing wake that you leave! You'll make your fellow sharks bawl! Your jet-action will slow them to a crawl Very green with envy and from your jet-stream, It is sure to make all of them steam!

---

[6] Play me for a fool.

Drink all of it down now, right here
Don't try to cough, and sneeze don't you dare!
Until you get in the water, well away from
here! For some might think its sea-weed and
algae. If near the beaches your jet appears!
Third time we meet is your bad luck, for I am
calling and giving all the shots! I'm quite
partial to shark meat, Next time you'll be quite
clean and lean! Just look at my pots, I've got plenty more! Now
that flying fish gone through - you get the score?

Begone all of you! To Hell whence you came, and continue
merrily to burn! I must to my saucily naughty dreams return!"
Crestfallen, shaking and shaken, from the room they quietly fled,
To seek cravener pastures that they might fill with dread!
Again she closed her eyes, and said to herself,
I really must hurry, so little time is left!
It's a good thing I'm so responsive and quickly off the mark!
I'm off to the races while it is still yet dark!
My jockey I've picked, tho' he feels he picked me.
He's a strong bare-backed rider, the only spurs in my hide,
is his muscled legs, strong sinews and once wounded pride.
Yet he keeps me busy, coming and going!

It's a good thing I buy pills wholesale and very cheap,
They sure give this girl some adventurous sleep!
Pacra[7] water they say, is a better, less expensive remedy.
I hope no one believes that, for to me it would be a tragedy!
My forté and my fortune are the patents, I sell one for every
malady, and the potions and the tonics that I make, bring home
the bacon, and put icing on my cake! Tonight I feel like having
something saucy, But not what I gave to the Shark to take!
He will be quite trim and lean, hungry like hell in Hell, and very,
very mean!

From the sauce out of that gander,
This goose will stay very far away
I won't go near sea-water for many a day!
There are a whole grappe[8] of others
To give me pleasure and sauce me with delight!
Hear the clarion call! Its time for the races!
Make the drums roll! Let the trumpets blare!
Races are for winning, I would like a victor's share!
But if I come first, or second, or even if I don't place
What really matters is how I finish the race!

I always enjoy dead heats, they're so very much alive,
With all the excitement of the pulsing, finishing drive,
The swiftly pounding beats of stout hearts and strong feet,
Building up pleasurable emotions quite hard to beat!
I call for more speed from the jockey up top!
How deliciously sweet it can be, When he has the strength to
respond, To that frenzied call from me!

---

[7] mollusc
[8] French for bunch

Faster he pumps, giving me the gun with his all!
Swifter I breathe, sucking air in great gulps
As fully stretched out for home we gallop!
Feeling the pressure of racing heart throbs
Reaching again for goluptious[9] air with great tearing sobs!
Faster and faster, we quicken the pace,
Two worthy thoroughbreds in a Great Race!
In those gloriously bruising moments, speeding at max,
To finish both first and last in a thrillingly sweet climax!"
Of organs and muscles near breaking point!

"Oh great happy joy! A pair well-matched!
They need only a brief rest
Before they start to gallop again!
This time as they trot gamely out,
It seems that they are already hearing the shouts
Of encouragement and welcoming praise,
For once more neck to neck they sweat and strain
As the jockey gives the horse free rein.

It may be the longer distance,
Or the effects of the Last Great Race, but this time the running is
more leisurely paced! Building slowly as they swing around the
bend, Both sense the agonizing ecstasy, Both call on deep inner
reserves, Until the sweet sauce of a photo-finish in deep
Warm-jetting arc to a delirious upward arch, Was the reward so
richly deserved! Happily quiescent they lie, chests slowly heaving,
Fingers caressing, lips skillfully teasing, While resting their tired
joints!

---

[9] Splendid, luscious

How many races were run that night, Or how many were lost and won, No one was keeping score! What is for sure, all were filled with such delight, That they kept going back for more!

The sauces from that gander pleased the goose so much, she took his phone number, So that she could keep in constant touch! She paid him to put in call-forwarding, Because she just hated on his call to wait! She wanted maximum time with delicious speed, For she truly dreaded delays, and being late!

For quite apart from her saucy dreams,
She had so many money-making schemes Either in the pot, on the fire, or just an eye-gleam, She sometimes got so confused and beat, About which one was to boil, To roast, to fry, or to broil, That she often got steamed from taking so much heat!

If she doesn't take things more leisurely, Relax, and enjoy what life has to offer, She will eventually, probably, suffer,
The fate of one being cooked in her own sauce! I bid you adieu, and hope you enjoyed The Night Tale tale of the garden and the impious elves, With sauces to make, to shake, to take in, to take out, or to jet! Please take your pick, and don't you fret,
For in all sauces you fortunately abound!

STILL IN LOVE WITH YOU

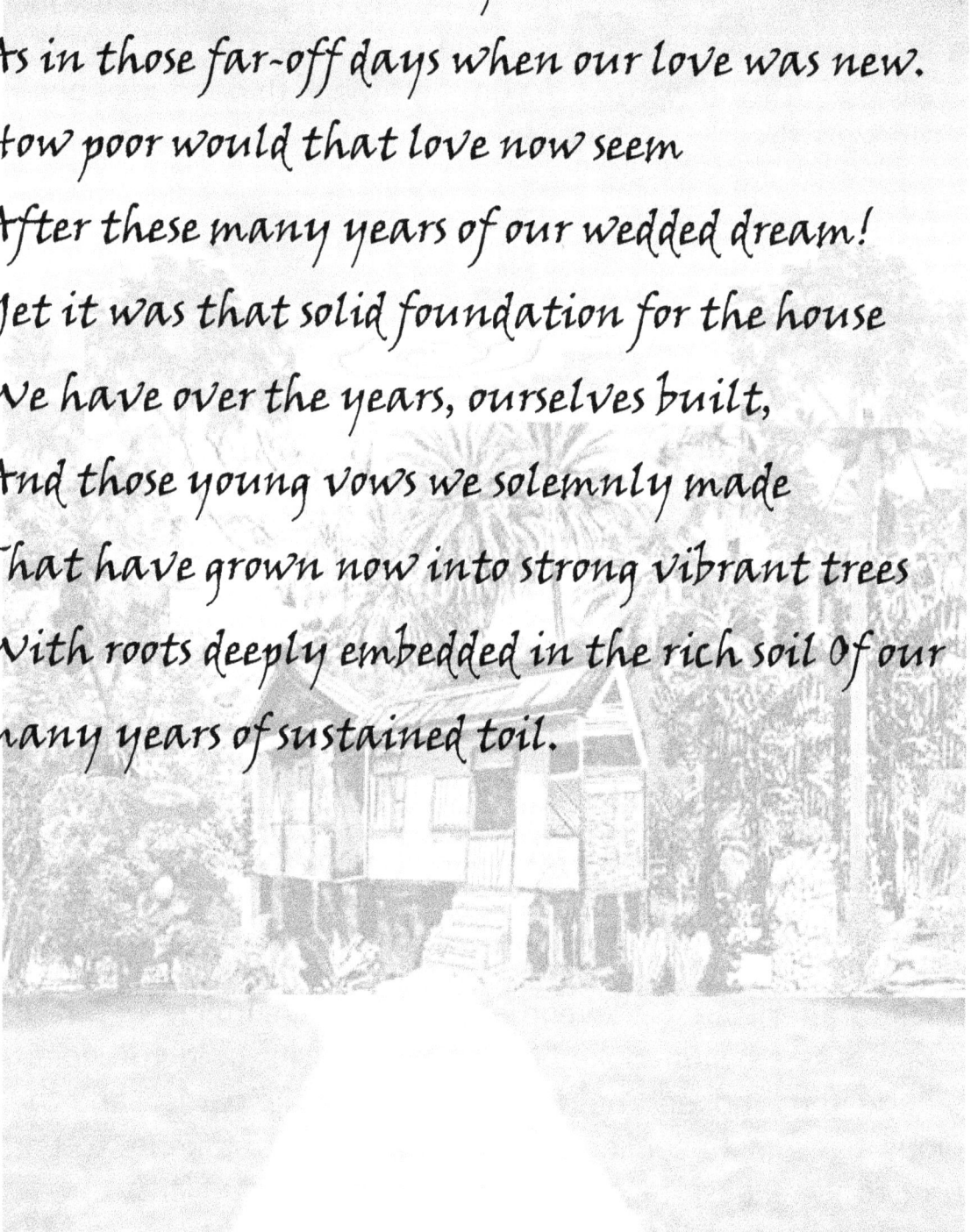

Were I still in love with you

As in those far-off days when our love was new.

How poor would that love now seem

After these many years of our wedded dream!

Yet it was that solid foundation for the house

We have over the years, ourselves built,

And those young vows we solemnly made

That have grown now into strong vibrant trees

With roots deeply embedded in the rich soil Of our

many years of sustained toil.

The lights from the windows now shine More
gloriously bright, while outside grows darker with
enclosing Night. And in that house of love we both
shall live, while our committrnent to each other
We freely give, Until the Spectre becomes a Firm
Reality!

The walls we built are comfortingly strong,
And the gabled roof we so lovingly placed,
To shelter us from stormy weather,
Has kept us dry and warm,
while we're still together.
The trees, the plants, the shrubs we planted Are
now sturdily strong, so the blossoms
And flowers show their colours all year long.
We have enjoyed the fruit and produce
From what we've sown

And marvel at the things we've grown.

Our mishaps leave us undaunted.

For we know that Life gives,

But there will always be a struggle

To o'ercome the problems and win the battle.

Some say we're on our second honeymoon

This statement I have always disdainfully

amended, That cannot be, the first has not ended! "

Now the hours do more swifly pass,

Since our children have left our home at last.

Together, and alone once more.

We are freed for now to explore

The many dreams and plans we made.

Very much like in those distant years before.

We live out our days in harmonious peace

Always conscious of Life's continual changes,

Content with the gifts we both have brought

To a life together which we happily sought.

For all those wonderfully happy years We thank

Our Almighty God Jehovah, Who with the Beloved

Son Jesus Christ, Has blessed us both with

continued And undeserving Grace.

He gives us daily The Sustaining Bread Of Grace

and Love. Flavoured with Forgiveness for our sins.

Through the Beloved Son we seek from God,

Happiness, Health and Peace of Mind.

For those three treasures are not easy to find!

And while a chapter of this book may be read,

There's always more to the Book of Life

When we pray ahead to the Divine Master

Who always knows what we need.

When that final bell shall ring, No mournful tears should it bring, No tolling bell, but happy chimes, And a hymn of thanks they'll sing To The Lord who gave us, Those many blessings over so many years. For in the memories and in the heart and mind Of the one that's left,

Fond recollections of shared happy times

Shall wash away sorrowful tears.

Smiles at memories will sweep away the fears.

At Nightfall!

Come, inspire me you Muses,
To continue from whence I left off
In telling the adventures of Moonbeam ,
At night in her many dreams. Full four weeks she allowed to pass,
And then to herself said, "This surely cannot last, I've not heard
from him at. all. Not so much as a call, To say 'How do you do?'"

I've just seen the sun set, as a prelude to the nightfall.
Soon will come the moon so bright, To bathe the land with silvery
light, And here I stand wondering, 'What's to become of me?'

Is this what's life all about? Just to rise, to dress, to drive to
work, Then drive back home again, To hasten into the garden
To perform so many chores, That I am truly exhausted
While the evenings are yet young! And these days are really very
long.

At nightfall to shower or to bath,
To eat and then to bed to go,
With all good intentions a book to read,
But tired eyes droop slowly low
More oft I admit, to words they do not heed!

Phrases, sentences, and paragraphs
Just make no sense to me. I close the book, and then my lids.
I settle snugly in...just to fall asleep!

Surely that's no sin? Am I not singularly free?
Why then do 1 feel so guilty
As tho' life's bypassing me?
Like a mouse on a treadmill,
All I see is hill, on hill, on hill!

No laughter, tears or voices
These rooms hear.. 'cept my very own
The only ringing peal is from the telephone
The Radio and the T.V, leave me really cold
On them I've no time to waste
They're never to my taste,
That I can endure them for too long
To listen for one hundred hours
For just one short, sweet song?

Sweet was the sound of silence
Which of late I do so dread.
I often wish that it be replaced
With children's chatter instead.
All I've got to look forward to
is sleep, perhaps dreams, maybe good health.
And studiously avoiding me is Love, Happiness and Wealth.

Even in dreams I've fared with little success, Small wonder then that I'm under so much stress!
Tonight I will try yet once again, But all the signs and portents indicate That it's surely going to rain! When it does, my dreams go so sadly awry,

It takes a lot of Will for me not to cry. I now lay me down to sleep, To dream of love..., perhaps to weep.
Come Queen, sing more songs
Let me know all my wrongs!
Visit once more I impelled,
On what's past I'll not dwell!
A night like this should not be wasted
When Pleasure's sweet cup's to be tasted!
Venture here good fairy, and sweet love
For you both I'll be a turtle dove
All honeyed sweet, peaches and creams
Just help me get to my dreams!
Without dreams a man is naught
Far more so is a woman distraught.
If to her, her dreams are denied,
And no lover is by her side,
To while away the hours,
And to court her with flowers!

"Come, Sublime Romancer once again
I'll speak plain, I miss you much, Your
mouth on mine, your tender touch
That caused my skin to blush sweet red,
When your hands strayed there instead.
Let me your sweet head caress
But bring me no gossipy messes.

I'll coo, and sing, and whisper sweet and
low, Love songs and love words that I
know, To please you. I'll tease you with
delight. We'll have ourselves a delicious
night."

Asleep at last, and off she
went, To visit the Land of
Contentment. Not on any
steed or mare, no magic
carpet in the air. these are
modern times I swear!

What she used had a tray at
back, instead of legs four wheels there were. The purring of the
engine noise replaced the hoof beats of the horse, And to keep
the beast on course. Instead of reins she held, another wheel!
'Neath her no saddle was there, Just a long wide-cushioned seat.
Doors and windows the great beast possessed to take away the
heat. Instead of neigh, a horn she pressed,
And it gave such loud a bleat, to clear the road, that as she
passed, Pedestrians white like sheet, jumped out of wits and skin,
So closely did she race!

For at the sound they looked,
And saw what was on her face.
Grim and determined look there was,
She was going a-visiting!
If Mohammed to the mountain will not
go, Then this mountain to Mohammed
will surely show its face!
I shall seek out the romancer's shack,
If he won't come to mine.
Should he be slow, I'll set the pace,
The pleasure will all be mine!
If he be fast, I hope he'll last..
It'll be a night divine!

Oh Queen Mab[10], direct this cab,
To where my lover lies, May he lie with, and not to me,
For that I cannot bear! To hear falsehoods no pleasure can I
derive. It's not for that I do right speedily drive.

I hope he's in good health and well rested,
For tonight's the night he surely'll be tested.
'Harry will tarry', said he,
"I hope that's no idle boast.
If for his mercy I finally beg,
I'll do it with great delight,
But first of course he must put up a fight!
We'll tilt, and list, and tourney,
joust, and all of that! We'll have ourselves a ball,
I hope to be one sorely contented cat
at the end of this journey.

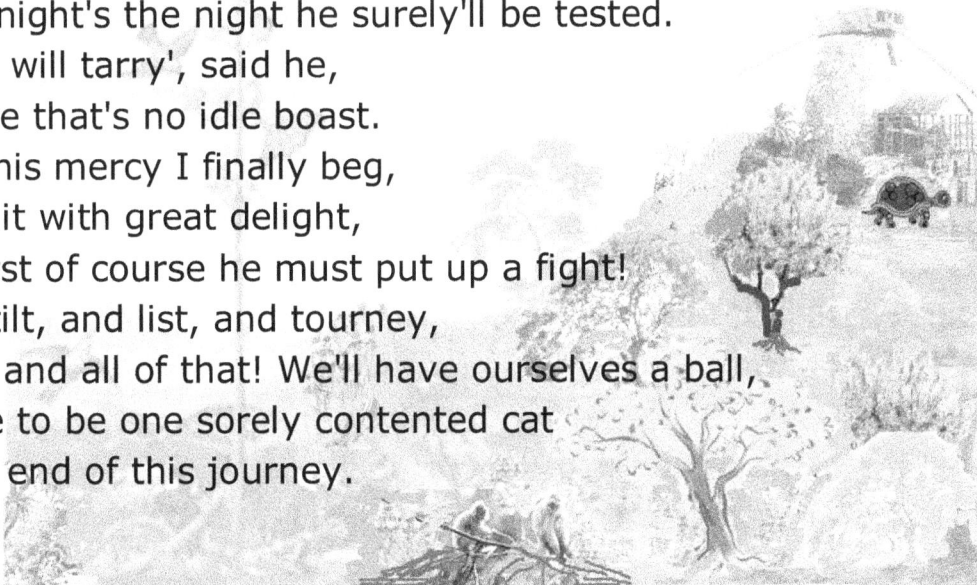

---

[10] a fairy referred to in Shakespeare's play Romeo and Juliet.

No sooner was this said, Suddenly came the rain.
"Oh no! Not Now! Surely there must be a better time for this
blessed rain to fall! I hope the romancer's roof is in better shape
than mine! Now just where he said his place was? This track, is
that it?.. straight up ahead!"

Through rain and wind to the door she ran Lowlight flashlight in
her hand. And with it she did bang ..on the door. He opened
slowly, eyes flew wide to see, Just who came in through the
downpour. "Oh, it's you!" he whispered throatily. He stood
shivering and forlorn, Like a lamb whose wool is shorn,
Then winter comes right suddenly.

"Listen, I behaved like a shrew that night, Please forgive me, if
that's all right. Just tell me what I've got to do, To make it OK
with you." "Well for a start, take off those clothes, Here's
something warm and dry You must have travelled through your
house, To get so wet through and through".

"I had that coming, I must admit but let's just cut all that.., out.
I've come to make amends, Hoping lovers still, if not, friends.,,
She hugged and kissed him Oh so tenderly, that he gave up his
peeve, To concentrate on the businesses in hand.

Then in earnest the tourney started, Rules invented as they were
needed. No hostile combat this, Tho' it was thrust, thrust, thrust,
and parry, While it lasted..... Dilly dallied, Harry tarried, Losers
none, winners both, Sore, happy, plighted troth., To meet and
repeat every other Night Fall. Why no oftener? you may quest. I
assure you it was at her request For she was always... very busy!
And he badly needed the rest!

LOOSE THREADS

The voice on the other end sounded distant. Distant not only in terms of miles, but distant in terms of years of silence and in terms of family relationships, shared trials and smiles. It was after all thirty five years later that this approach was being made so hesitant. In thirty five years the water under the bridge has been diverted over many courses. New families are established, babies grow up to get married and to have their own babies - and parents, uncles, and aunts have passed on, or are in the waiting room not knowing their departure time, or knowing it, seeking means to delay the forces. But blood is thicker than water, and water under the bridge is water that has already gone through, so the happy surprise and the warmth in the voice of the one being called suddenly clears the line and lessens all the remources.

He wishes to visit for a while, to meet with other members of the family whom he knew once, and to get to know those of whose existence up to this time he has been unaware. (And quite possibly uninterested, I may declare). But the phone is only the medium for re-establishing and acknowledging the existence and the importance of familial ties, and he will be arriving on the seven o'clock flight on Wednesday next, so please prepare. He is coming alone; for two weeks ago he buried his wife in Canada. And now the pieces are failing in place. "Forsaking all others, until death do us part, amen and amen, gone with grace."

After thirty five years the reasons for the rift have been obscured and overlaid by more important memories, but those who have no memories are unsympathetic and impatient, "No, I am not going to the airport to meet him - no way, he's been too distant! He is your brother, and that makes him my uncle, but that is all that he is to me - my father's brother, no special other. He is not my Uncle! Show me the cards he sent for my birthday or that he sent you for Christmas. Let me see the pictures of his family, or didn't he have one, the old carbuncle?"

"Yes I'll be polite and mind my manners after all he is a stranger and that is how you brought us up - to be polite to strangers. But don't ask me to run and kiss him, I will feel like a hypocrite. Can I say that I have a virus or a dispirit? Yes, that is a white lie, not a true lie. If you want me to tell him the truth I will say that I had better things to do with my time to rearranger."

Blood and curiousity win the day, and the size of the welcoming party will please a Sheikh, far less a relative until the mêlée with all the introductions. The missed names and the dropped faces, the mix-up with the porter and the other stranger, put reconciliations in danger. "He not only old; but he dotish!" Said in retaliation to the perceived insult exchanger.

"Yes uncle I've been a good girl" - but why should you care, you have not been here! What about your kids, uncle? Are they good children, tell the truth dare?" Where are they and why aren't they with you? Are they too busy or too busy to come here? Don't they care? It would have been better if they had come, for they were not at fault, and they are closer to my age it's true."

"Grandchildren you say! My! My! Do you send them cards or do you visit thereby? So she was on a kidney machine that long? It must have cost you a bundle or is the health care support so strong? Thirty three years of marriage to the same woman, and you miss her you say? "

.,,, I wonder if any one will miss me after thirty-three years of marriage or more to the point will I miss them or care, or would we have fallen asunder?"

"You brought pictures! Oooh! look at this one, she looks like grandma.... Why that was grandma's name, she still reads her scripture...And this boy here... He looks like Reggie - excuse me, Reggie is Aunt Myra's son. ...You know Aunt Myra she is still there. Uncle Theo died four years ago. They were so close that even now she says she can't wait to see him again, time now passes so slow. They were married thirty two years.... I feel soooh sorry for her you know. .,.What? You were married thirty three years,.., Feel sorry for you too?" .....But that's different. .I don't know you, and if I don't know you how can I love you as I love Aunt Myra and loved Uncle Theo, it's not so easy to do. He was so ,,,alive! He made you feel glad to know him,,, and to be near him. If I miss him so much it must be hell for poor Aunt Myra to have lost him.

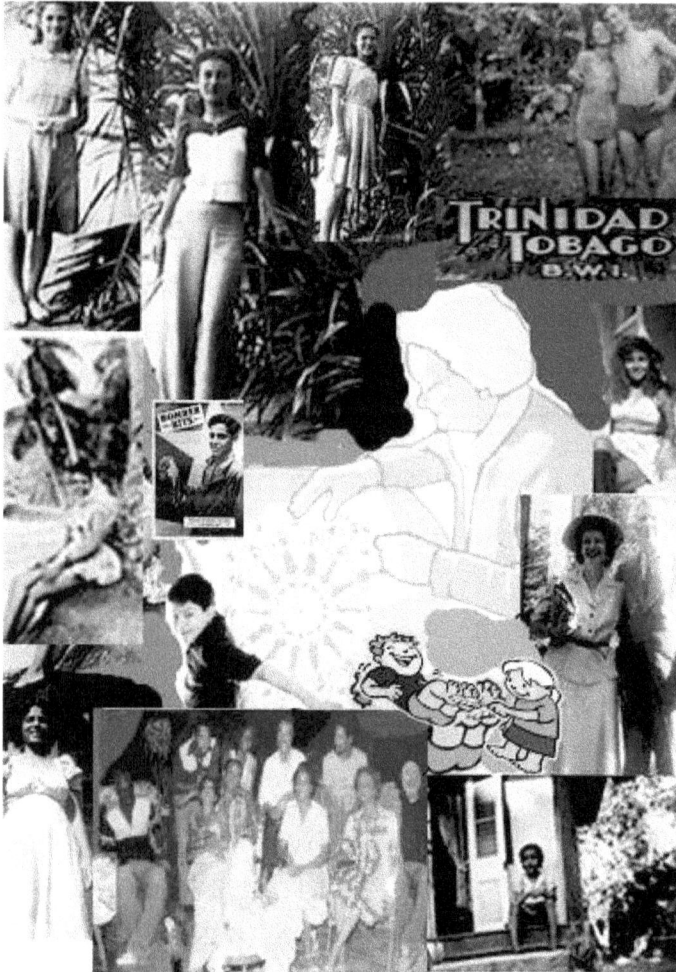

But uncle this is a picture of Rupert when he was fifteen! He is away now in Germany. He got a scholarship, and you know what? I don't think he will come back here,,.,..
This place gone through that's what they always say! .....

What? It's a picture of your son Andy? ..Well I never! They took so alike, who would have thought?

I'm sure to fool Mummy with this one .. She's in for it this time...Not even knowing her own son! "So that is why you left thirty five years ago? You felt the same way?"

Well things are not so bad here after all because after thirty-five years ...... we still waiting to go through. Yes.... this our house we are coming to now.. .It's allright... it ain't too bad it hasn't given us too many tears. You think so?".......Mummy will be pleased! Welcome home, Uncle Reggie, and I do hope you came for a loooong stay!"

THE SONGS OF SILENCE

Come, sing sweetly to me Songs of the Sounds of Silence;
Sounds of the greening of leaves in the trees;
Songs of the Sounds of flirting flowers
Singing to busy birds and buzzing bees.

Sing *cantilena* the soft melodies raindrops hum,
As they seep slowly through parched earth.
Sing songs about Sounds tiny seedlings make
When they sprout through rich, moist dirt.

Sing of Soundless Sonatas created
By milk drops falling in the Milky Way.
Sing of *decrescendo* Celestial Symphonies
The distant stars compose, as they swiftly move away.

Tell me where do all the lyrics go when they leave the comets tails?
Lull me to sleep with the sweet lullabies
The Moon sings to the skies as she sails.

Let me hear gentle*vivace* music of Light
From the quietly Dawning Day;
Sing *rallentando* songs of the velvety-soft darkness,
As the setting Sun silently slips away.

Sing *pressisamente* of meteors and meteorites,
Marking their bright swift paths as they burn.
Sing *giocoso* jingles composed by the lovely Rings of Saturn.

Sing sweetly and tenderly *amoroso*

Love-songs about Silent Venus;
Of secret undying promises that were broken;
Trill Songs about fulsome praises from lips that have never spoken.

Sing me *The Canticles of Silence* from the lips of unborn babes;
Of the Presidents, the Kings, and the Queens,
The Poor, the Rich, the Famous, and the Genius,
The millions of the *"The Might-have-Beens"*
Who have never seen the Blessed Light of Day.

Sing of all of their hopes, of all of their dreams,
Of all of their futures, all so cruelly thwarted.
Sing mutely of parents who have caused
Their destined lives to be aborted.

Whisper sweet Sounds of happy laughter
From the lips of friends I have not made,
Let me hear the beautiful music from the tunes I have not played.

Sing loudly songs *alla marcia* of heroic struggles on Mars.
Thrill me with songs *calando* about rusting weapons of Wars.
Sing softly *staccato* of unfought, tumultous Battles,
And of all their fearsome scars.

Play in reverent silence music *allargando*
From all our answered prayers;
Sing of the pure golden-honey Sound
In the Sweetness of unneeded, unshed tears.

Enchant me with verses sung by nests of young fledgling birds.
Sing Songs of their Silence when nestlings are no longer heard.
Sing of long-moulted feathers quietly falling, bumping, *"boop!"* to earth.

Entrance me with songs *affrettando*
Of the Attini, or leaf-cutting ants climbing with determined purpose

While waving large green umbrellas in their programmed dance
To and from their fungi farms.

Sing of the Soundless cry of the needle
As the thread pierces its eye.
Sing of the cloth quietly screaming
When the needle drills through its ply.

Your songs *dolente* of the Sounds of swiftly fading flowers
Will always bring tears to my eyes;
So sing only a few to flavour slightly this silent Fest of Song!

Sing songs *adaggio* of letters from friends who did not write;
Hum faltering dirges about brave fallen warriors who ne'er did fight.
Sing songs *largo* of Sounds on The Paths We wished we had taken;
Sing songs of the fond Hopes, of the many Dreams we have all forsaken.

Sing songs *adagio* of the Sound of melting ice cream;
Or of the quiet sound of stagnant water in a dried-up stream.

Sing me some songs from all the many secrets
That empty houses always have to tell;
Of those quiet lonely Sounds of avidly listening walls
In rooms where people no longer dwell.

I love the way you sing your songs,
I feel their warmth, and I relish the subtle humour in your twinkling eyes;
For these are the songs to which we sung along
In those far-off years when we were both fresh and young.

The Song Cantabile of Silent Time
Now hums ever louder in our ears;
Now, we sing songs *grave* of swiftly on-coming Sounds of Age,
Drowning out the songs *allegro con brio* of our once-youthful years.
Now, it matters little if we sing off-key,

Or if we forget the tempo, the tune, or the words.
For We Know we sang them very well with Glee,
When we were gay, young birds.

We shall somewhat later hear The Sound *dolente* of the Silent Song
That other silent*Thief* sings, as *He* stealthily sneaks our lives away.

But *should I die*, and a tear is heard
As it seeps slowly down some one's cheek;
The Sound in the Silence of that unspoken pain,
Will tell that the lives we lived were not in vain;

For we have sung, we have lived, and we have loved,
We have dared to face the many Heartaches,
We have fought all Life's Struggles,
We have shared Life's sweet Hopes, Life's great Joys,
And Life's bitter Sorrows.

And my life found such Love in a heart
Which now so silently cries,
That the sweetest Song of the Sound of Silence
Is the One that I never heard!

But should*You* be trapped within the cobwebs of Death,
Before I have ended my appointed Day;
If*You* fall prey to His *All-consuming greed;*
Then even louder and sweeter
The Songs of the Sounds of Silence will play!

For when I look at the flow'ring plants,
And at the lovely blossoms of the trees;
When I pray silently, on old grieving, aching knees,
When I perceive the silent distant stars
Quietly traversing the great heavens above;

THE GOD I PRAY TO

The God I pray to is not a Sunday God, who sleeps for the rest of the week.
The God I pray to is always wide-awake, and His Blessings and His Grace I constantly seek.
The God I worship is always in my thoughts, every hour of every wakeful day.
Before I go to sleep at nights, to Him on my knees I pray.

The God I praise and glorify , is no Monday God, awakened for one hour on that day.
Then to be thrust aside, allowed to sleep, 'til next Monday comes,
Or some unforeseen, calamitous day!
The God I sing my praises to, looks not at my shoes and my clothes,
But deep in my heart, through hidden recesses of my mind.
To see if my deeds for that day were always good and kind,
And that the words of contrition I use are truly sincere.

The God I pray to is not a Tuesday God, Whose Presence on other days I deny.
He is the God I think of, and pray to, on all other days, whenever and wherever I feel so inclined.
I bless and praise His Loving-kindness, His Wonderful Gift of Redemption, purchased for us,
Through the Blood Sacrifice of His Son.The Innocent Lamb, so that we may forever live
In perfect peace, when we are once again lifted from Earth's dust.

The God for Whom I look Heavenward, to plead for His Forgiveness and Sustaining Grace,
Is not a Wednesday God, Who listens and blesses me only on that day.
He is the Always-Present God who is busily giving of His Grace, each day in every way.

There is no Thursday God for me, for The One that I know and I trust
Is always near to hear my prayers, and to guide me on the Right Way.
He forgives my sins, showers me with Blessings, His Love and His Grace
He has always been to me, infinitely kind and He breathes gently on my face.

The God I know and pray to is no Friday God,
He is the One and Only God for me.
He is the One I shall follow wherever He Leads, whatever my destiny.

And what about the Saturday God?
Where and how can I place him, when I know in my heart and my mind
The God I acknowledge and trust, the One I must pray to, think of, and love,
Is with me every minute, of every hour, of every day of the week.

He is truly The Living God of the Sabbath, and of every day of the week.
His Son, our Blessed Saviour, sits on the Right of His Fsther's Glorious Throne.
It is Their Blessings, Their Love, and Their Saving Grace, that I must always diligently seek!

I know that Our Redeemer lives, and He and His Father, Almighty Jehovah God,
Shall reign with Supreme Power and Glory,
Every day, every week of every month of every year,
Through All The Ages, and throughout Eternity.

TODAY I PRAY FOR POWER

*Today , I pray for **Power**!*
Power, not to rule the World, the Nation,
or even my village, but *Power over myself!*
I pray for the Power of Faith to help me
overcome my weaknesses and my fears.
I pray for the Power to Overcome selfishness.
I pray for the Power to be Able to make
the best use of my life on earth.
I pray for the Power to Speak wisely,
and with conviction.
I pray for the Power to Forget my hurts,
real, or imagined.
I pray for the Power to Love,
to Forgive those who have hurt me.
I pray for the Power of Peace of mind.
I pray for the Power to Use my mind
and my will to heal my body.
I pray for the Power of my body to be strong
enough to support and nourish my mind.
I pray for the Power to Love unselfishly.
I pray for the Power to be Patient when things
go wrong, or I am displeased.
I pray for the Power of Perseverance to work
towards making them right.
I pray for the Power to Guide my family
on the Right Paths.
I pray for the Power to Enjoy
all the good things in my life.
I pray for the power to Endure and to Rise
above all the evil and corruptible things
to which I have been exposed.
I pray for the Power to Make people happy
when they are in my company.
I pray for the Power of Laughter,
to lighten whatever burdens life may impose
on me.

I pray for the Power to Resist temptation,
and to Avoid Sin.
I pray for the Power to Remember, and to Pray
for those who have helped in my journey
through this life.
I pray for the Power to Look into the eyes
of people, and to See the good in them,
no matter how deeply it may be buried.
I pray for the Power to Think things through,
and to Arrive at the correct decision.
I pray for the Power to Act on those decisions,
and to see them reach a proper conclusion.
I pray for the Power to Enable me to walk
the Path of Righteousness,
so that I May continue to find Favour
from Almighty Jehovah God.
I pray for the Power to Use all my talents
in His Service, and Most of All,
I pray for the Power which comes
from His Blessings,
For that is the greatest Power that I can have!
For without His Blessings, His Love,
and His Grace, all my prayers would be in vain!
I pray for the Power to Use those Powers
wisely and for His Glory
I pray to receive these Powers
through Our Saviour, Jesus Christ.
If all my prayers are answered, I shall even
more earnestly pray for His Help, His Grace,
His Love, and His Blessings, for without them
all my Prayers, and all my Powers will be dust
in the wind, a ripple in a swiftly moving stream,
or an inconsequential decibel, forever lost in the
noisy traffic of life!

K.I.T.Lans
95.02.19

REFLECTIONS

How peaceful it is to sit quietly and to see the sun go down at sunset! That great ball of fire moving slowly down to the horizon as though to the water's edge to be quenched for the night. No hiss is heard, nor billowing steam seen as it disappears from view. But he, the sun, is not finished yet – not by any means – for in defiance of the night, and as a promise for to-morrow, he lights up the sky and the high clouds behind him as he departs.

The normally swaying coconut trees are very still. They are watching, standing rigidly at attention, as though in silent and formal homage to their departing emperor. Well they might, for they are very aware that they owe their continued existence to the life-sustaining light of his presence.

The sky is suddenly alive with soft and vibrant pastel shades of red, golden-yellow hues interleaved with blues and browns. The blues are the clouds hovering very close to the sea, thus mirroring the shade of blue they see. They seem to be asking to be re-united with their parent.
I fantasise that she tells them no, not until they have reached the utmost heights, traversed the distant lands, and have done their alloted work. Only then....not before.

It is a beautiful and touching scene, painted by the Master Painter on His great canvas that is the sky. A dynamic painting, ever-changing with both subtlety and high drama. Heightening the sensation is the loud crashing of the waves on the rocky shore line. A *Son et Lumiere* performance by Nature. They are all original performances by the same actors, improvising wth sublime effortless ease on the accustomed roles they play. Today, these are no gentle waves lapping on a golden sandy beach, spent for a moment by their previous efforts. These are implacable invaders, hostile and mindlessly dangerous. Their advances and their efforts sound like cannons firing salvo after salvo. They are the shock troops, heard as the sea renews its eternal quest to take the citadels of stone by force. Waves of Sound and Silence, of Light and approaching Darkness, signal the closing of the day.

The twittering birds add their harmony to the concerto's finale as they scud across the sky to roost and to nestle for the night. I sense more tranquillity in the notes they warble now, as if they too, have put aside the hurried tensions and the cares of the day to the morrow still to come. The frogs interrupt the melody with their discordant throaty refrains, sounding very much like those unfortunates who need to cough during the quiet passages in the performance of a symphony, thus completely spoiling the effect for which the conductor and orchestra had so carefully worked. The crickets not to be outdone, shrill their presence for considerable distances. Amazing, when one considers their size.

The waves come in now with increasing force at nightfall, as if tonight is the night that the walls will fall, but the rocks hold back the enemy with resolution, for surrender means dissolution and shatter-scatter, to be ground slowly and inexorably into sand and dust. The irressistible force against the immovable object. Eventually the sea will prevail, for its warriors are ever changing, and after every wavy encounter fresh troops attack at several points with constantly varying intensities, while the rocks remain defenceless, resolute and steadfast, slowly and imperceptibly giving ground, by eroding under the continual assaults.

Water, wind and sand are the allies against this indomitable object, and during the day the sun joins the alliance and the attack, adding its heat to the fray, forcing cracks, and forging fissures which are invaded by the unmindful enemy.

There is no retreat or respite for the rocks, and they have no defence against the onslaughts.
Incredibly their only chance of survival is to grow! Yes, to grow out of the path of the mindless wave and the traitorous sand so lately a part of the steadfast rock. To have then only the wind and the sun to continue the attack. And this they will. They surely will. They too eventually will win the unequal

contests but at an infinitely slower pace than before.

Can we take a lesson from all this and apply it to ourselves? What changes may be possible if our only chance to save ourselves from attack and defeat was to grow! Surely sometimes that is also our only chance to escape the relentless waves of destructive emotions, feelings and habits that seek to destroy us even when we wish to stand firm and resolute as the rocks? To grow morally, spiritually, intellectually. To give ourselves a better and longer chance to be constant and steadfast.

We are more fortunate than the rocks, for *We Have the Ability* to be as *mobile* as we choose. We all have some responsibility also to leave for even one fleeting moment every day of our lives, a little light behind! A light of enjoyment and of peace that signals yes, today we came this way, and that for this – oh so very brief moment – we did liven up a portion of someone's sky, and gave some measure of tranquillity. How wonderful it is to know that we will do the same thing to-morrow!

K.I.T.Lans
92.05.24

THE COLOUR OF HOPE

How does one colour Hope?

We hear about a person who is crimson with rage. Another may be blue with melancholy, and still another may be in the stygian blackness of deep depression. But doesn't one get white-hot with anger? Isn't the bird of happiness be-decked with blue plumage? And speaking of birds, isn't the bird of peace portrayed in feathers of white? So with all these confusing palettes, how then should we paint Hope?

I like to think of Hope as being rainbow-coloured. I think of its shape as being defined by the arc of the rainbow. It is an arc with two beginnings and indeterminate dimensions, the limits to be decided and to be set by ourselves.

These feelings may have been fostered by childhood readings of the story of The Great Flood, and of God's Covenant with man. It was the first symbol of Hope to me, and on almost every occasion when I feel that I am getting depressed, I look to the skies, and there, for me to see and to enjoy, is Hope, the blessed forerunner of things to come!

What happens on the few occasions when I do not see it in the heavens? Fortunately, I have learnt to look elsewhere for other things which help to overcome those dangerously negative feelings. Although they may be all man-made, they seem to me to be Heaven-sent, and they convey the same message. There is nothing profound about them, and indeed others may regard them as trivial or mundane. Those 'other things' may not even be noticed by others.

On the road as I travel, I see a mother and her teenage daughter walking, side by side, on the road in front of me. The teenager is holding with the barest of touches, her mother's finger, and in that gesture I read love and understanding, trust and mutual respect; for as I go past, there is no indication as to which is the leader. Their talk is animated and friendly. They are obviously enjoying each other's company. There is no generation gap here; I feel comforted, and my spirits lift.

Further on I see another mother, this one is waiting with her son, to see him safely into the maxi-taxi which is to take him to school. While they wait, he is busily engrossed in playing some little game with his feet. His mother is looking on, but she is not really watching. Her thoughts are far away, but she seeks the comfort of knowing that her son has been safely despatched by her to school. He is young enough to accept her presence without resentment or embarrassment. Unlike the other two, they do not talk or touch, they are about their own business.

But they share a common purpose.

I come towards a little girl sitting astride her father's shoulders, bouncing along, one hand clutching an ice cream cone, the other grasping for security, any part of her father's face which makes her feel momentarily safe. They both look happy, for he is humming a gay little tune, and he is as unmindful of the ice cream dropping on his shirt, as she is unaware of the damage being done to her dress from the melting goo which slips through her sticky little fingers. Occasionally she takes a lick. She is very conscious of how far she is above the solid earth. Her face is a mixture of delight and caution, as she responds to her father's song and the bumpy ride. I hope for both their sakes that they do not have too far to go.

Once more I see the colours of Hope.
They are blended with the colours of love,
warmth and trust, affection and understanding.
The darker hues of introspection and temporary isolation serve only to enhance the picture, a picture which is unconfined by a frame.

All around me there is evidence of these rainbow colours which are so deeply ingrained in the National Pysche.

I think again that there is no end to the Rainbow of Hope. The beginnings are always glorious to behold!

Hope is a wonderful experience, to be coloured anyway we wish, so long as the colours radiate the warmth and the light to make us feel happy with the road it illuminates before us.

It is a road which we ourselves can light as brightly as we desire. or which we may leave as sombre as we want it to be.

For the switches are all within us, and we can become expert at lighting our way, or at cursing the darkness of our own choosing, as we grope our way forward, unwilling to use the tools we have, to make our journey through life an invitingly pleasant one.

NOVEMBER'S LAMENT

The caged dog's mournful howl signalled
November's lament at Winter's steady approach.

The luckless lady, bouyed by the happiness
of Spring,
Followed by the brilliance of Summer's rays,
Could not face the cold reality of lonely
Winter's reign.

For her lover's insistence on impending Changes
Meant long-feared rejection of Spring's
blissful Moments,
And revived all the half-forgotten torments
Shallowly buried in the grave of Bitter Memories.

Rejection swiftly yellowed into dejection,
Icebergs of dark depression shattered
Her tenuous hold on life!
Now she perceives how the leaves more swiftly
fall,
Regardless of fulfillment of purpose,
or of ripening Age.

She sees that the love-birds and their young
have flown from branches fallen silent,
still leafy, but yellowing-green.

No buds, no blossoms, no flowers are seen
On the Poui trees which had previously given
So much pleasure.

Once-warm wind grows slowly chill,
Through her ever-deepening gloom it seems
All Nature conspires to make her ill!

Oh, the unimaginable agony the Mind
Sometimes cruelly inflicts,
Only those who have experienced know
and fear!

Sharper than the surgeon's knife,
With hurts more cruelly painful
Than any that the body is made to bear!

Oft it leads to thoughts of escaping Life
by a desperate door,
Because it foresees an eternally dark future,
With no vestige of a warming Light!

The Distraught Mind forgets
That Dreary Winter always passes,
Giving way once more to Cheery Spring's
Freshly-greening delight.

Against that burgeoning mental pain,
No salve nor unguent can relief gain.
Life's past sweet pleasures or Memories' treasures
Are no surcease to tortured feelings
Striving for everything to remain the same!

Cast adrift, alone, with only dark
and stormy seas ahead,
She felt that No One had ever truly cared!
This one, like all the other Promised Lands
Had proven to be unbearably unreal!

No silvery romantic light
Nor golden sunshine of Reality
Could pierce that increasingly dense black fog!

Abandoning Hope, Faith, Family, Friends,
Even precious Life, and the future ahead,
She sought refuge in Death instead!

Oh what a **Waste** of Life, of Hope,
To spurn the chance to Drink of many other cups!
But bitter, tortured minds do not reason,

Forgetting their Faith in **His Divine Love**

They are lost in, and feel only unendurable,
Unending pain!
They suffer their self-hurts so intensely,
That they feel they can no longer go on again!

We continue to be comfortably blind;
For if our eyes could truly see,
They will perceive that the same can easily
happen to **You** or **Me**!

But *That* is so unnerving to contemplate
We prefer our lids to be closed and our lips to
prate
About the illogical stupidity of such *felo-de-se*.

What do we *know* of the hurts or the distress
That gives a fragile brain no rest?
So overloaded with ever-increasing stress,
It finally chooses self-oblivion as best!

We may never know the answers,
Nor how to ease those crushing hurts,
But it tells us to be more alert
To all the possible dangers we will surely court
When we choose to walk where we wish,
Heedless that sometimes it leads to Nowhere
But to Lost Hope, Shattered Dreams, and Utter
Despair!

Oh if we can only turn, retrace our steps,
Until we meet some other avenue or lane
Which we had ignored while speeding to a Stop!
Then to step briskly down this new-found road
To see what other brighter future it can hold!

An old Love's Dream died,
But so too has *All the Past!*

We can once again give ourselves the Chance
To explore and savour all that lies ahead!

To Live! to Smell! to Hear! to Feel! to See!
To give ourselves those other future days
To Enjoy Whatever Vistas Other Lands may
offer.

Truly on the Road unfolding through *Our Life*
We **should not** seek out **Death**!
We are sure upon some Destined Path
He lies somewhere, a-waiting us!

But until that Certain, Chancy, Final Meeting
We should see what else is in store for us,
Whether bitter, very sweet or only fleeting!

We should live Life to it's fullest
Until we cross that Great Divide
To the End we all must meet.

The **anguish** of our future days **There**
We have no means of knowing.
We surely know that if it is worse
We have no way of returning!

So let's All pray to Our Good Lord
That no cup we taste should be so bitter
That we cannot see His Light,
Or that we forget His Ever Lasting Love.

While Age presses down, with eyes growing
dim,
We fervently ask that our Faith, our Hope,
and our Love,
Continue to **Light the Way** to **Him**!

Teachers at the Forest Reserve Primary School, including Mrs. Eulaline Lans.

I HAVE A LOVELY GARDEN

I have a lovely garden, which I carry around in my head.
I visit and work there very often, especially when I'm in my bed.
I have a lovely garden, in which I diligently tend
To all kinds of different beautiful shrubs and plants, in elegantly ordered beds.

"What grows there?" You may well ask, as you question my sanity.
"All sorts of things, and wondrous plants I have collected over many years.
They are ideas, thoughts, and plans of action to be taken or deferred,
Memories, cherished or bitter-sweet, to which I constantly refer.

I water them with my imagination, and they are nourished then with my prayers.
I give them frequent talks of encouragement, to show I really care!"
This I reply to questions asked of me.
I do not feel I'm hurting anyone, and all my labour is free!

I have a lovely garden, it is my favourite retreat.
From all life's noisome stresses, and its sometimes unbearable heat.
I can stroll through shady avenues, under trees I instantly grow.
I shrink and expand its limits to all the degrees I know.

I may strew the paths with flowers, to enjoy the fragrant smell.
I can tell the trees to blossom, and like magic I see the blooms swell.
Then one stroke of my magic wand, I will make them all disappear.

I have a lovely garden, in which no chemicals are used.
There are beds with names I chose to fit the plants that I try not to abuse.
"I'd like to do," "I like doing," "Things that please me," "Helping Hands,"
"Dreams and visions," "Pure Fantasies," and many more to numerous to call.
And in a remote shaded section there are some called "Weeds."

"Why 'Weeds'?" "What on earth for?" "This is crazy!"
I can hear you say out loud.
To which I give my counter with this most logical reply.
"Weeds you will always have, whether you like them or not.
That's certainly no lie!"

I grow them quite separately, and harvest them before they seed.
I plough them into the soil with all the discarded, unfruitful ideas,
Along with other bitter herbs that frequently appear along the Way.
I try to keep them under strict control, so they don't get out of hand
And it is a challenge to get some better use from them whenever they show their heads.

They provide a sharper focus when I see them as I pray,
For they are called, "Self-pity," "Malice," "Fear,"
"Doubt," "Selfishness," "Temptation," and even "Sin."
All are stubbornly hardy perennials, striving to control The Way.
I zap them with my Prayer-gun with which I keep my garden secured.
I have a lovely garden, and one of my favourite spots is "Helping Hands."
For I can stroll down Memory Lane to see the shrubs, the plants and the trees,

THE TIME I HAVE

Yesterday is gone, so I no longer possess it.
Therefore no longer have I the hurts or the sorrows, the fears or the cares of yesterday! Freed from them, I can more readily pursue my hopes and my dreams. I can explore and expand the limits which I, and no one else, have imposed on myself.

Yesterday's value today can only be derived from the use I make of the experiences I gained from living it; from what I have earned in tranquillity and peace of mind; from what I have done towards achieving the goals I set myself on that day, and the closer relationships I have made with everyone with whom I have had contact, and my relationship towards Jesus Christ and Almighty God.

Yesterday is History now, and I shoud use all my experiences of that history to guide me to lead a better life today.

But what do I really have today? I cannot say time, for no one possesses time! Time is not a commodity which can be traded borrowed, stolen, or sold.
We cannot kill it or waste it.

Time gives!
It gives us the valuable asset called Opportunity.

Opportunity is an asset which we can use, abuse, squander, and refuse if we so wish.

Tomorrow is the Future, and only Almighty God knows and owns that time. He alone controls the Past, the Present, and the Future.

Tomorrow!
I can plan for it, I can dream of it.
I can even delude myself by thinking that it is there for me.

Such delusions are only useful when they allow me to use my abilities, to develop my talents, and to enlarge my capacities for self-improvement.

Today's opportunities provide the keys that we can use to unlock the doors to the future.
That future we can control to some extent by our choice of the keys presented to us.

We should always be cognisant that there is some value attached to the ones we have not chosen, and thus we should carefully weigh all our options before making our final choice.

Tomorrow is a goal!
We should strive for it, but never take for granted that it is there, waiting for us.
We may be closer to reaching that goal when we live better lives today than we did yesterday!

THE PRAYER LESSON

I was somewhat surprised the other day
To hear a young wife sheepishly say,
"I don't know how to, I cannot pray!
When I try to say the words
They jumble up, and I get confused!"

This she said quite eloquently
To a friend she had met only recently!
I wondered what she had done as a child,
Had she forgotten "Gentle Jesus, meek and
mild?"
Or all those sweet nightly prayers we were taught
When we were just young tiny tots?

Jehovah God Almighty is our very best Father
/Friend.
Of His Great Love and Understanding there is
No End.
Prayer is conversation with That Good Friend
Whom it seems, we often unwittingly,
Sometimes willingly, offend!

Like any other friend that you have wronged
For reconciliation you must firstly make amends.
So at the beginning of all your prayers
You express contrition, or regret sincere
To remove the stumbling-blocks of your guilt,
doubt, and fear.

Then you bless and thank your Friend Jehovah,
For all His Blessings. His Loving-Kindness,
Mercy, and His Grace, the Gift of Redemption
That He has bestowed on you and the whole
human race.
Call and bless the name "Jehovah God
Almighty!"
With feelings of love deep and true,
To be sure that He is listening to you.

Assured now of His Forgiveness, and His Great
And Merciful Love,
Ask for the things you want or need,
And be sure that He will pay you great heed.

Pray not for fame, property, or wealth,
But for Peace of Mind, Happiness,
and long-lasting Health.
Ask for the warm security of His Abiding Love
For continued harmony at home and work,
Blessings like-wise for all family and friends,
And all the other precious spiritual things
More valuable than ivory, silver, or gold.

Then lay your problems one by one
On The Greatest Problem-solver, bar none.
Comforted and eased by your lightened load,
You ask Him to show and keep you on the Right
Road.

To ensure that all you said is heard
You ask it All in the Name of His Son, Lord
Jesus Christ,
Our Blessed Saviour, Lamb of The Great
Sacrifice.

Have your husband and your children kneel with
you,
And use words and phrases that they know,
For in the eyes of Jehovah, Almighty God,
We are all children too!

Then hug and kiss them tenderly,
To show your love for them and The Almighty.
You will be refreshed with feelings of Joy and
deep Content.

Continued daily contact with Your Almighty
Friend,
Gives access to unlimited power without end.

Prayer can be idea-thoughts, words, sung or
said,
Prepared writings that can be read.
Snatches of hymns, or Bible texts.
It matters little, for He understands every format
and each context!

Pray briefly as you go about your daily tasks,
And never be afraid of Him to ask.
Remember however, that like all loving parents,
He, Jehovah God Almighty, sometimes says,
"No!"
For no earthly reason you can perceive,
But be sure there is a Heavenly One,
You must believe!

We pray to Jehovah, Almighty God,
Not because He needs our prayers,
But to maintain a close Relationship
With The One we hold quite dear.

No set routine of words, stance, or time of day,

A House To Z!

There in the road we lingered to chatter
about this, and that, and some other matter,
with a mother still proud of her handsome son,
while laughingly taking him to task.
Then there came a knight rider
who stopped right beside her,
to ask about Freddie's house!

'Is that it?' he queried, pointing
to a roofless structure fifty feet away.
"I'm afraid not, it's right next door,
just about to be started nearly any day!"

"But surely there's some mistake!
Fred spoke at length and so convincingly
of a dwelling that is almost finished!

"When I look about, and then around
I only see near virgin ground
where sweat or tools ne'er fell!
Just what can I poor Fred tell
when I see him next Wednesday?"

Puzzled at our carefree laughter
He turned to me and said,
"Surely you there can tell Fred
What you know is really going on?"

"Have faith," I replied, "and soon
you'll see his tall and handsome son.
In that wooden shack over there he has the latest
in electronic gear.

"Unless Fred doesn't have his number,
why should he be call-waiting to hear
what progress he's making?
If his father wants instant contact his son

has a telephone and fax!

"Call-forwarding, and fax are not toys,
all he has to do is call on his boy
to report what he's done!"

More puzzled now than before,
shaking his head in wonder
The Knight looked at the house-less land,
Then once again at the laughing band
standing near to his rented car.

"They seem to be holding some secret ace,
they are in such festive mood.
With no real start on the place,
This surely is a time to brood?"

His bewildered eyes asked the questions,
While he thought of what next he should say.
Slowly shaking his confused head,
He said, "Instead of a report from me,
Freddie himself should come to see
What he has described so lovingly.

A self-styled graduate from the University
Of Universal Good Common Sense
He may find here what I surely cannot see!
Maybe I'm just uncommon dense!"

Looking again at the topless house
Where work had ceased for over a year,
He sought again to allay his growing fear
Before he left for that other shore.
This time he addressed the son
To find out what was the score.

"How long before you complete

Your father's dream in which he
Has invested his life savings?
I thought for certain that building
There was poor Freddie's dwelling!"

In a flash, with debonair and great dash
The answer came right speedily back,
"Two months and one-half,
Maybe a little more perhaps,
It has to be done before December."
Turning and looking straight at me,
He added quickly and laughingly,
"Of this year for very certain sure!"

Then said his mother, "If Freddie came to see
his house,
after what he has spent, with shock and disbelief
his clothes he will rent, his hair he will tear!
And he'll work himself into a rage!

He would not come, for that very fear
with all his carded "A to Z" degrees!
Instead he sent me to check and report,
then to comfort and put him at his ease.

I leave this place tonight by boat
Although I've not yet bought my ticket!
I have no idea what I can say to him
That would not take his wicket!

I may take for him to read some verses
on his predicament,
Hopefully in them he may find some words of
cheer, and even merriment!"

Shaking his head with despair and great dread
the knight rider changed his gear,
while looking at the virgin land in fear,
with his rented vehicle he slowly disappeared.

Next morning in sunlight bright,
back once again came he.
"I'm leaving today and I came to see
The kind of work that is going on.
This is my third trip this sunny morn

Yet I saw not a trace of Freddie's son!

I dread to think of the awful great stink
his father will make of the money wasted
One hundred thousand dollars,
is what he stated he has forwarded to his son!

And except for that shack
so far nothing at all has even begun!
What meets my eyes when I gaze around
is only bush and weeds a-plenty;
Not even a fowl run, after so much money!

His father will be in great distress
to learn that what remains to be done
is just everything!
For he fully expected that the roof
was all that was needed,
before tackling the finishing touches.

The poor old chap asked me to check
how near was the completion date
of the house of his lifelong dreams!
I dread the thought of hearing his screams
when I relate the sad fate of his vision,
and say it was just an expensive illusion!

But friend Freddie should not fret
For goats do not sheep beget!
And gauvas and limes are not the same,
though both are yellow or green
with plenty seeds!

The son is a true, true block
straight from Freddie's stock!
Nice to have met you, ...but I really must go ....
For today I must leave for home!"

He then departed with a heavy heart
burdened by conditions that he must impart
when he next met his Savannah friend
as they both jogged around the track.
And I could not help the awful feeling
that someone's future suddenly went **black**!

A Thank You Note!

I have read the lovely book you so thought-
fully sent
And awaited the inspiration that you meant
That I should receive.

But, Alas and alack, this country hack
Has yet to feel a flicker of what you brought
When you were here earlier this year.

I looked at the lovely postcard with tulips
Artificially place-ordered in sombre profusion
But alas and alack, this country hack
Had to look for them very close to the ground!

I am sending you some pictures
Of what God's gift of blessed rain has wrought
An Easter's parade of poui flowers
Stretching from Earth to Sky.

They covered our garden in such profusion
It looked like pink Tobago snow.
And for once all the trees were blooming,
A truly wondrous feast for the eyes to behold!

But alas and alack, this country hack
Mourns the blooms quick demise.
The trees have turned leafy green, however,
Despite the drought that is now settling in.

We're sorry you missed Cheryl.
She came home the week after you both left.
But alas and alack, she has gone again!
Back to the University of Waginengen

Wewondered at the glories of Ireland,
Wewere touched by the Irish pride
Of their native land.
But alas and alack, it saddens us
That they also took pride in killing
Their fellow Irish men.

We enjoyed the Irish poems immensely
We felt the thoughts and the dreams
They conveyed, but alas and alack,
I got the impression of a wearisome sadness,

No doubt because they feel somewhat
Displaced In their own Island,
And perhaps even betrayed.

We hope Märyke's elbow is better
And she's walking with a steadier gait.
I hear that it is difficult to do so in Ireland,
Because of their Guiness which flows
Unabated, with good and merrisome cheer!

We hope you enjoy the pictures
And see what you both have missed,
But don't worry or feel sorry,
For there's no guarantee when it'll happen,
So we enjoyed it while we were lucky!

We hope that you are both in the best of health
Enjoying the best of your heavens' offerings,
While being happy together
Through rough times and smooth seas.

We here in the isle of Tobago
Have learnt to relax and enjoy what we have.
We wish for nothing more than for good
Friends who will visit and stay
For a while longer next time.

We wish you content of mind and good health
May you continue to enjoy your untold wealth
With peaceful and merry hearts.
For one never knows when the weather'll
Change.
Or when folks and/or fortunes will drift apart!

Once more we thank you most sincerely
For the wonderful gifts you have posted.
We are happy indeed they arrived safely
For us to read and enjoy happily.
We're glad that they did not get losted!

I'm sending this to your Dutch heaven
And we wish it will safely arrive.
Please let us know that you are both happy,
Contented, and still glad to be alive!

www.ingramcontent.com/pod-product-compliance
Lightning Source LLC
Chambersburg PA
CBHW080533030426
42337CB00023B/4720